THE RAIN

FOREWORD

INTRODUCTION

THE MIRACLE OF A RAINFOREST

DENIZENS OF THE FOREST

PEOPLE OF THE FOREST

THE RAINFORESTS IN PERIL

Published by Smithmark Publishers
112 Madison Avenue
New York, New York 10016

Produced by
Brompton Books Corp.
15 Sherwood Place
Greenwich, CT 06830

ISBN 0-8317-7342-1

Printed in Hong Kong

10 9 8 7 6 5 4 3 2 1

FORESTS

TEXT   D'ARCY RICHARDSON

FOREWORD   RANDALL HAYES
            RAINFOREST ACTION NETWORK

SMITHMARK
PUBLISHERS INC.

INTRODUCTION

A tropical rainforest is one of nature's greatest spectacles. Venture into a rainforest, and you enter a world defined by varying shades of green. In an area the size of your backyard, hundreds, perhaps thousands, of plant and animal species thrive on plentiful rainfall and constant temperatures. These species have evolved over millions of years to produce an ecosystem more diverse and complex than any other on the planet. Over half of all the species on Earth make their homes in tropical rainforests, which now cover only six percent of Earth's land area. From the fungi on the forest floor to the towering trees of the canopy, a rainforest is populated by some of the most fascinating and spectacular life forms on Earth.

Tropical rainforests form a green swath around the Earth's waist, from the Tropic of Cancer in the north to the Tropic of Capricorn in the south. The largest areas of intact rainforest occur in the Amazon Basin of South America, the Congo (Zaire) Basin of west-central Africa, and the Indonesian-Malay archipelago of Southeast Asia. The remainder of the rainforest is scattered through Central America, the Caribbean, Hawaii and other Pacific islands, Australia, the Southeast Asian mainland, India, Sri Lanka, East Africa, and Madagascar. Tropical forests grow in the regions that were left uncovered by glaciers during the last Ice Age. Although their species composition was affected by the changes in precipitation and temperature, the forests continued to evolve into their present forms.

Tropical forests aren't the same all over the world, but vary with geographical regions, elevations, and soil types. The species that make up the forest on the seasonally-flooded várzea along the Amazon are different from those of the cloud forests of Colombia or the heath forests of Sarawak. By the same token, a lowland forest in Brazil will harbor different plants and animals from its African counterpart. Wherever the rainforest, however, water is always abundant. Rainforests require at least 80 inches of rain annually, with the wettest areas receiving over 400 inches.

The most marked feature of a tropical forest is the interdependency of all its creatures, and the very specific niche each species fills in the community. In response to intense competition for limited resources, the plants and animals of the forest have developed highly specialized techniques for survival. There are rainforest crabs that eat only coconuts, and fig flowers that rely on one species of wasp as a pollinator. An orchid in Madagascar hides its nectar six inches down a narrow tube, so that only the long-tongued hawk moth can reach it, pollinating the flower at the same time. A flower in the Amazon gives off a scent like that of a female wasp, so that as the male of the species tries to mate with the flower, he gets covered with pollen. When he is fooled again, the pollen is transferred to the next deceptive flower, allowing the plant species to reproduce and survive. The most amazing facet of this incredible dance is that the flowers bloom during the one and only week when the males are waiting impatiently for their female counterparts to hatch out of the ground. The hollow-thorn acacia tree provides food and shelter for one species of ant, who in turn protect the tree by stinging unwanted animal intruders and destroying any plants nearby that are competing with the acacia for a space in the forest.

There are insects that mimic other animals, or even plants, to protect themselves from predators. A certain caterpillar resembles a snake, and a species of praying mantis looks just like a pink orchid flower. Tasty butterflies protect themselves from birds by dressing in the garb of their less palatable cousins. The forest is full of these bizarre and wonderful creatures, each heavily dependent on the others for survival.

What we humans have come to realize in recent years is that we, too, are

THE MIRACLE OF A RAINFOREST

From above, the canopy of a tropical rainforest resembles a green carpet stretching for miles, broken only by the towering crowns of the emergent trees. This lush, green growth is the pinnacle of a long evolutionary process in the tropical regions of the world, a process that has produced half of all the species on Earth.

Scientists theorize that what is now the tropical region of the world was much drier during the Ice Age, causing the lush forest to shrink into isolated islands where there was still enough moisture and a constant enough temperature to support their growth. The original species composition of these islands was similar, but when they became separated they evolved in different ways. When the Ice Age was over and the islands were once again joined, the number of species had multiplied by the number of different adaptations each island had produced.

The diversity and lushness is obvious to anyone who spends time wandering in a rainforest. What is not obvious is that this lushness springs from a virtual desert. The soil underneath the towering trees and blossoming orchids is hardly richer than what you might find in the Australian outback. Geologically speaking, the tropical areas in which rainforests grow are very stable. Without the regular upheaval of new bedrock and its subsequent breakdown through weathering, there is no new supply of nutrients and the soil becomes old and nutrient-poor.

The secret of the rainforest is that its plants are experts at reusing almost everything that falls to the forest floor and decays there. The plant roots form a dense mat over the soil. When leaf litter and animal remains begin to decay on the forest floor through the action of fungi and bacteria, the roots quickly snatch up nutrients that are released in the process before the heavy rains have a chance to leach them out of reach, deep into the ground. Once the plants have the nutrients stored in their tissue, they retain them by developing thick, waxy leaves to prevent further leaching by the rains. This difference is apparent when tropical forests are compared with colder, temperate region forests, such as occur in most of the United States. While an oak forest may store as little as 10 percent of the available nutrients in living tissue, or biomass, a tropical rainforest will typically store 70 percent of all nutrients in its biomass. Because of this ability to retain nutrients, the forests can thrive on very poor soils.

And thrive they do. At every level of the forest, another world unfolds. Layer upon layer of vegetation culminates at the canopy, where it explodes into full bloom. Most of the action takes place one to two hundred feet above the forest floor, where trees blossom and bear fruit, and animals come to feast on the bounty. Water evaporates from the leaves, rises, and forms clouds that later return the rain to the forest. A full 50 percent of the rain that falls has been recycled from the forest itself. The dense root mat acts as a sponge, retaining the water and allowing it to be released slowly into the many rivers that have their headwaters in the forest, thereby preventing devastating floods downstream.

Ecologists, climatologists, botanists, and a host of other scientists are still struggling to unlock the mysteries of the tropical rainforest. While they continue to examine the many parts that make up a rainforest ecosystem, we can marvel at the beauty and complexity of the whole.

15 The graceful arc of Wailua Falls drops out of lush rainforest in Kauai, Hawaii. Rainforests thrive on high moisture and constant temperatures, with the wettest forests receiving over 400 inches of rain per year.

16-17 Peruvian forest slopes toward the Amazon Basin, which contains the largest area of intact tropical rainforest on the planet.

18-19 The canopy of a lowland tropical forest stretches as far as the eye can see in Borneo. Lowland forest is the most complex and diverse of all tropical forest formations.

20 The forest canopy is broken by an oxbow lake in the Venezuelan jungle. Early perceptions of the rainforest as an impenetrable mass of vegetation arose from travelers' experiences on the waterways, where an increase in available light allowed for dense undergrowth along the shore.

21 *Flame trees bloom near the edge of the Daintree rainforest in Queensland, Australia. Flowering plants are so abundant that the intense competition for pollinators has led to very specialized relationships between plant species and their pollinators.*

22 A river is dwarfed by imposing crags in a South American rainforest.

23 Iguazu Falls stretch over two miles as they join rivers in the jungle near the Brazil/Argentina border.

24-25 Rainforests continuously recycle moisture. Here, mist lingers above the forest in Corcovado National Park, Costa Rica.

26-27 A stream rushes past a large-leaf philodendron in the Hawaiian rainforest. Forests act like sponges, protecting watersheds upon which people downstream depend.

28

28 The flowers of a dwarf poinciana brighten
the forest. Many rainforest species are familiar
sights in temperate zone greenhouses, where
orchids, poinsettias, and other tropical flowers
are sold.

29 Every inch of available space in a rainforest
is used. Mosses and epiphytes grow on tree
branches and derive their nutrients from material
that falls from above.

30 Fungi thrive on decaying matter in a temperate rainforest in Olympic National Park, Washington.

31 Tree ferns have survived since the days of the dinosaurs. These giant examples of our familiar ferns are abundant in the rainforest of Hawaii.

32-33 A Pandanus grove provides an excellent example of stilt roots, which tropical plants use for support and aeration in areas that are sometimes flooded.

34-35 A spectacular sunset on the Amazon River silhouettes the Peruvian jungle.

36 The delicate curves of these tree buttresses provide extra support for an arboreal behemoth in the Papua New Guinea rainforest. Rainforest trees characteristically have shallow roots, which are able to capture nutrients from decaying matter before the rain leaches them from the fragile topsoil.

37 Gnarled lianas store water and nutrients in their convoluted stems. These specimens are in Costa Rica's Monteverde rainforest.

38 Lianas, omnipresent tropical vines, creep up a forest giant in Peru. Lianas use tree trunks as ladders to reach the sunlight of the canopy.

39 Most of the activity in a rainforest takes place hundreds of feet above the forest floor in the canopy layer, where sunlight and food abound. The towering giants of the emergent layer rise above the dense canopy, capturing a clear advantage over their neighbors in the quest for more sunlight. This view of the canopy in bloom is in Costa Rica.

40-41 Delicate balance is required to guide small dugouts through the waterways of Papua New Guinea.

42 A tangle of ferns and mosses blankets the limbs of rainforest trees.

43 The bright petals of Amranon curazao grace the Panamanian forest floor. The tree produces a delicious fruit, locally known as the custard apple.

44 Strange forms abound in the rainforest. This fungus, Dictyophora duplicata, produces a foul-smelling liquid at its top which attracts flies. The flies unwittingly disperse its spores, which are contained in the liquid.

45 The decay of these leaves in a temperate rainforest in Washington State ensures that the next generation of trees will find sufficient nutrients to support their rapid growth. Without the continual recycling of nutrients, rainforests could not flourish on the thin soils of the tropics.

43

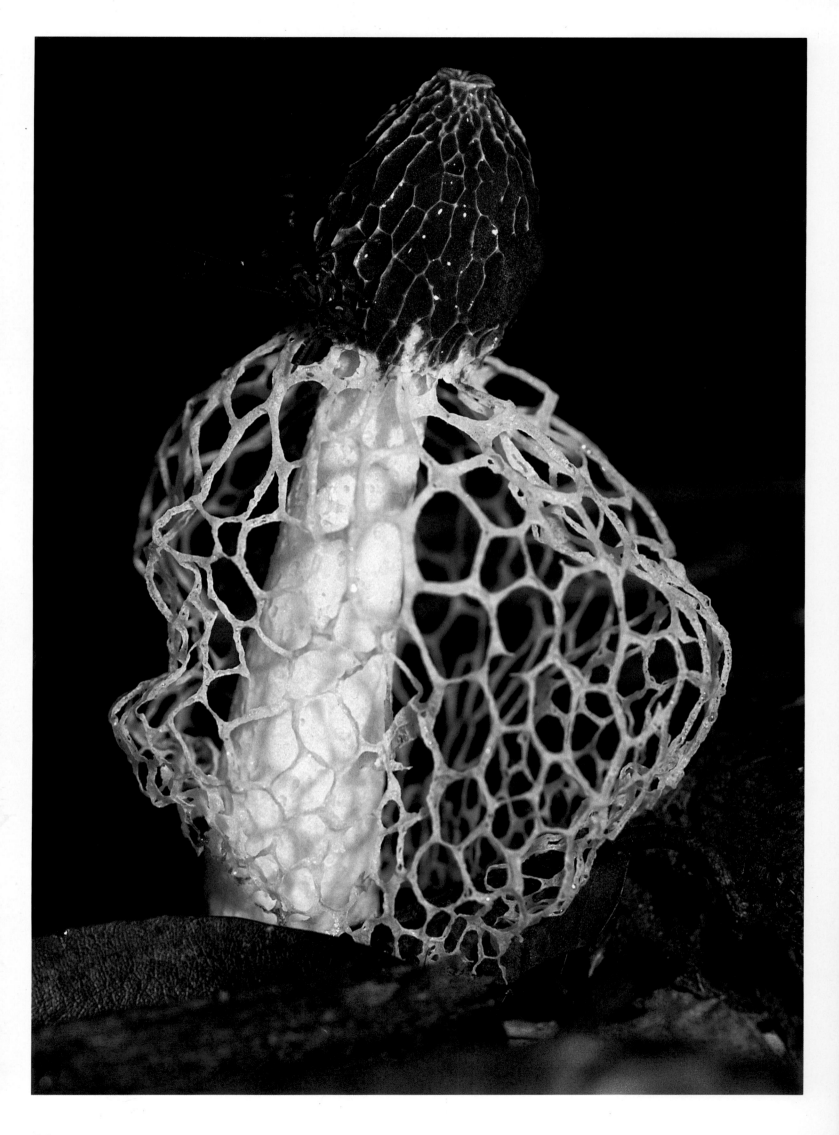

44

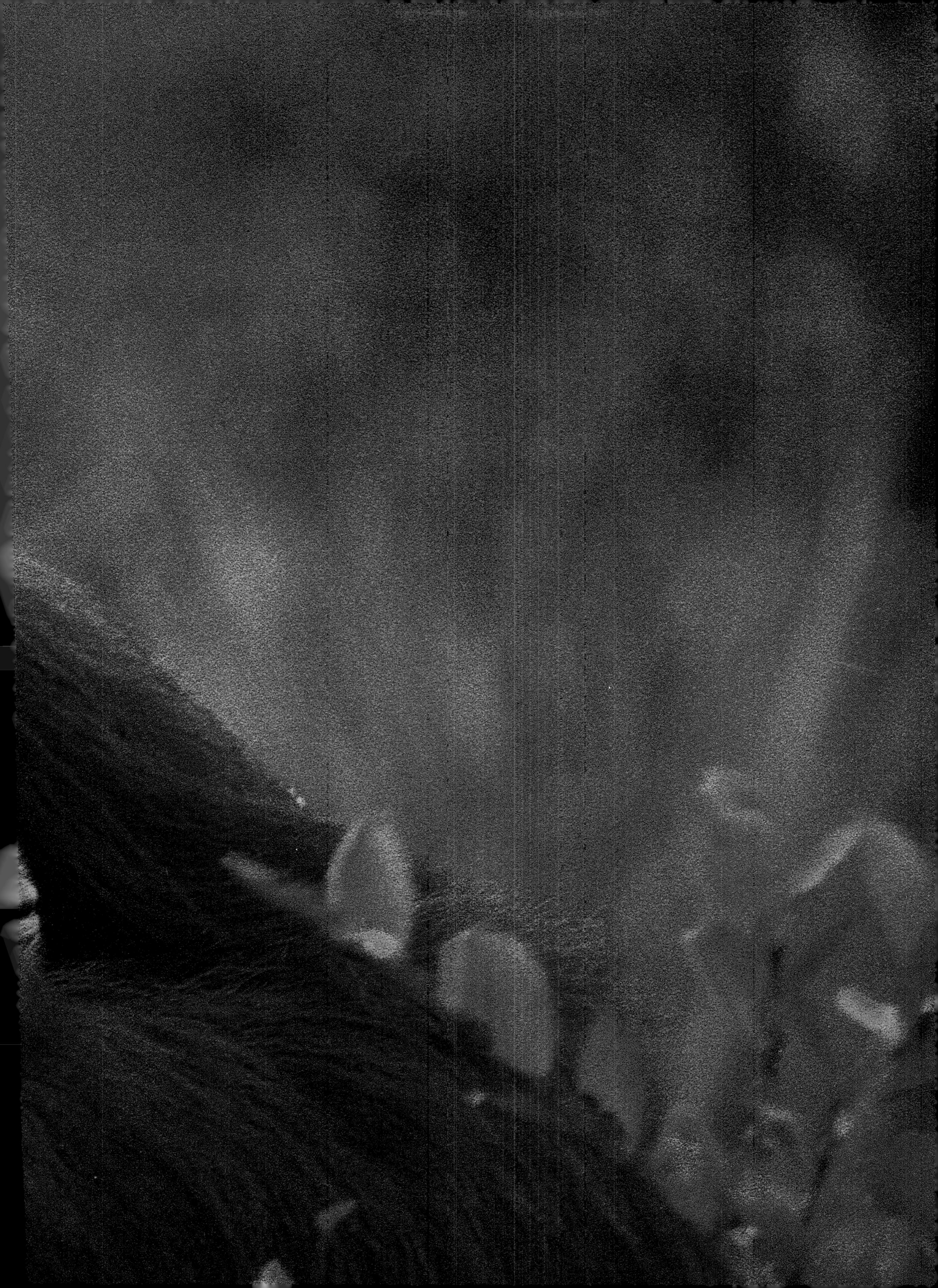

50 Orchids are a familiar reminder to temperate zone dwellers that the tropical forests of the world hold a fascinating variety of plants and animals.

51 The intricate patterns of an orchid species are crafted to attract pollinators. Some orchids have patterns on their petals that can only be seen in the ultraviolet end of the spectrum, invisible to the human eye.

52 A bright flower trumpet helps attract pollinators to this epiphyte in the forests of Costa
Rica.

53 A pink bromeliad is another tropical plant
that has become a familiar houseplant. A large
percentage of bromeliads grow on tree limbs
as epiphytes. They catch water and needed
nutrients in their characteristic water 'tanks,'
formed by the circular pattern of their waxy
leaves. The tanks make perfect pools for the
small frogs and salamanders that often inhabit
them.

56 Poinsettias originated in tropical climates,
but now they brighten Christmas around the
world with their red flower bracts.

57 One of many species of wild ginger offers
up a spectacular blossom to passing pollinators.

58 Giant Victoria lilies float on a river in Peru.
Known to reach over seven feet in diameter,
they are strong enough to serve as a small raft.

59 A giant fig tree in the Daintree rainforest in
Australia sends down a curtain of aerial roots to
the forest floor in search of additional nutrients.

60 Rare birdwing butterflies are found only in
Southeast Asia. They include some of the
world's largest butterflies, with a wingspan of
up to 7.5 inches.

61 Hundreds of different Heliconias offer a
myriad of bright, wax-like flowers that are
prized in arrangements for their color and
durability.

62 *Two spices in one fruit, nutmeg and mace are produced from the same species. The mace comes from the red, net-like seed casing, and the nutmeg comes from the seed itself.*

63 A colorful bunch of cashew fruit goes to market in Brazil. The fruit, which grows on trees, is highly perishable; the nut is the only part of the fruit that outsiders are lucky enough to taste.

64 *A spider perches in the center of an accomodating flower, jealously guarding her egg case from predators.*

65 *Colorful plumage helps parrots and other rainforest birds attract mates, but also attracts the attention of human predators.*

66 This toad is camouflaged to blend in with the Peruvian rainforest floor. Camouflage protects many forest creatures from their predators.

67 A tiny Peruvian tree frog clings to a branch. Many of these frogs have homes in the pools of water collected in bromeliads high above the forest floor.

68 This coconut crab in Papua New Guinea survives solely on coconuts as an adult.

69 An intricate spider web awaits unsuspecting insects in the jungles of Costa Rica. Some spiders can catch small birds in their sticky nets.

70 A crocodile cuts a fearsome figure near the
Daintree River in Australia. Crocs and caimans
inhabit many of the waterways in tropical rainforests, but poaching continues to deplete
their numbers.

71 'Chicken of the trees,' an iguana perches on
a tree branch. These reptiles are an important
food source for the people of Central and
South America.

72 The sloth's furry coat is well-adapted to its
upside-down ways. The hairs grow up from the
sloth's belly toward its back, allowing rain to
drip off quickly.

73 The mountain gorillas of Rwanda in Africa
face extinction because of habitat destruction
and poaching.

*74 A tapir looks up from its lunch in Belize.
Tapirs and other mammals are an important
source of protein for jungle-dwelling humans.*

*75 The king of the jungle in the New World, the
jaguar is one of the world's most beautiful cats.
Belize has recently set aside a protected area
dedicated to preserving prime jaguar habitat.*

PEOPLE OF THE FOREST

The landscape of a tropical rainforest is composed not only of its myriad plants and animals but also of its people. There are hundreds of forest cultures that continue to live in much the same way as their ancestors did, with a deep appreciation for and understanding of the benefits that their natural surroundings provide. The forest plays a central role in their cultural heritage as well as in their daily lives. Their respect for the natural world is reflected in complex rituals and mythologies which often portray the forest and its parts as spirits or deities, worthy of special recognition.

The vast majority of rainforest societies have spent their time learning to work subtly with the natural rhythm of the forest, rather than developing intricate methods of manipulating it. They know when certain fruits will ripen, and when the best time for planting manioc is, so they plan their routine to coincide with the forest's natural schedule. Many villages are only temporary settlements: When agricultural plots wear out because of nutrient depletion, or food becomes scarce because of overhunting, the people will move on to let the forest recover, perhaps returning many years later. While some people may view forest cultures as primitive because they lack the sophisticated tools and trappings of our modern way of life, they are in fact far more advanced than we are in their ability to function in their natural surroundings. A Yanomami hunter in Brazil may not have a rifle with which to stalk his dinner, but he knows that the poisons from certain plants or the gland of a particular frog, applied to the tip of his blow gun dart or arrow, will produce the same effect as the white man's bullets.

Indigenous cultures around the world know more about the plants and animals of the rainforest than even the most educated scientists. The peoples of the Amazon Basin count approximately 2000 different plants in their store of pharmaceuticals, many of which have yet to be analyzed by science for their curative properties. Modern ethnobotanists are racing to learn all they can about how the WaiWai of Brazil, the pygmies of Zaire, the Penan of Sarawak, and countless other cultures use the forest to treat their illnesses, before that knowledge is lost forever. Forest cultures are disappearing, and with them, the chance for us to learn more about the world in which we live.

Rainforest peoples find their world increasingly threatened by modern development. As the modern world penetrates deeper and deeper into the forest, the indigenous societies are confronted with mounting pressure to assimilate into other cultures. Cooking pots, guns, and clothing become new objects of desire, and young people cease to learn the important lessons their parents have to teach them.

Contact with the outside world has produced disastrous results for many cultures. Exposure to the unfamiliar diseases of outsiders, even those as seemingly innocuous as the common cold, have caused whole villages in the jungle to die. Cultures clash as modern man moves into the forest to exploit the resources upon which traditional cultures also depend. But indigenous cultures are beginning to fight back. The Penan of Sarawak have resorted to blockading logging roads on their ancestral lands. Peoples of the Amazon Basin have united to try to force the Brazilian government to recognize their rights as separate and unique cultures. And the Kuna Indians have turned some of their native land in Panama into a nature preserve, deriving income from tourist dollars while preserving their forest heritage.

77 A WaiWai Indian of the Amazon Basin bears trappings of the modern world. Traditional societies find it increasingly difficult to preserve their cultural identity from the onslaught of Western ways.

78-79 *Taro fields in the Waipio Valley in Hawaii are a poor substitute for the lush forests that these lands once supported. Forests in Hawaii face pressure from housing development, agriculture, and geothermal projects.*

80 *A dugout plies the waters of the Brazilian rainforest. Rivers are an important source of protein for native cultures. The Amazon alone contains about 2000 species of fish.*

81 *A young boy is perfectly at home on a tiny raft in the Colombian rainforest.*

82-83 *Sugar cane replaces rainforests in Central America as settlers strive to make a living from the thin tropical soil.*

84 An En-yeh-pah Indian of Venezuela displays a colorful macaw. Tribespeople often use bright feathers as body decoration during festivals.

85 Family ties are central to the structure of many forest societies. Elders are held in high esteem, as their knowledge is vital to the survival of the village.

86 A Huli wigman shows off the body painting for which New Guinea tribes are famous.

87 Kundu drummers in full regalia take part in a celebration in New Guinea. Many forest cultures' celebrations center around the forest and their relationship to it.

88 An elder near Port Moresby, New Guinea displays a traditional festival costume befitting of his position in the tribe.

89 A Gumine boy catches a ride with his mother in Chimbu Province, New Guinea. New Guinea natives are especially fond of body paints, and create intricate designs from naturally-derived pigments.

90-91 A family in Guyana stands in front of their all-important canoe. Rivers are often the only transportation route through the jungle.

92-93 A house on the edge of the forest in
Guyana is a typical home for peasants who
move to the jungle in search of land.

94-95 Testimony to one of the world's great
civilizations, a Mayan temple at Tikal in
Guatemala rises out of the surrounding jungle.
For a time, Tikal was the center of the Mayan
world, providing living space as well as cere-
monial centers.

96 Kuna girls of Panama sit in front of the colorful embroidery they sell to passing tourists. The
Kunas are the first indigenous people to estab-
lish their own nature preserve on tribal lands.

97 A Kuna Indian woman displays her native
garb.

98 A Peruvian quenches his thirst with the
abundant water stored in a liana. Lianas are
important sources of water in areas of the
forest that lack clear running streams.

99 A rubber tree is scored for the collection of
latex in Brazil. Rubber tappers' sustainable
use of the forest provides a good example of
how natural forest can generate steady income
for forest dwellers.

100 Son-in-law of the village witch doctor, this
Jivaru Indian of Peru is an expert blow gun
maker. Skilled hunters can hit prey from a dis-
tance of up to 50 yards.

101 A farmer harvests a cocoa pod from the
Costa Rican forest. A favorite of the Aztecs and
a native of the New World, cocoa is also produced in Africa, where Ghana now claims the
title as the world's largest producer.

102-103 The Dyak people of Borneo are an
agricultural society, judging the right time to
plant their rice by the position of the stars.
Dyak villages consist of large wooden long-
houses that shelter three generations of a family.

104-105 A family slips through waters their
ancestors traveled on the island of Borneo in
Indonesia.

108-109 Peasant farmers in the Mexican state
of Chiapas watch as the forest goes up in
smoke. Clearing for subsistence farming is still
the largest contributor to deforestation
worldwide.

110-111 Another scar is left on the forest as a
canopy tree is prepared for hauling. Selective
cutting is difficult in the rainforest because of
the many vines that link trees together.

112 In India and other parts of Asia, elephants are used to gather forest logs.

113 Increasing mechanization of forest clearing operations has contributed to rising rates of deforestation. In some areas, a chain dragged between two bulldozers fells large areas of forest in a very short time.

114 A worker marks logs for transport to a mill
on the Sebuku River in Borneo.

115 A lumber mill near Manaus, Brazil processes wood from the Amazon jungle. The Amazon has become Brazil's version of the Wild West, with boom towns springing up around the mines and mills.

116 A dead sloth clings to its tree branch,
reminding us of the interdependence of all
forest creatures. Habitat destruction through
deforestation is the primary cause of species
extinction in the tropics.

117 Scientists have discovered that many animals, including birds, are reluctant to cross
over even small clearings in the forest such as
this one. Clearing restricts the animals' normal
ranges, and may cause local extinctions when
food becomes scarce in isolated islands of
forest.

118-119 Once trees are cut down, the fragile
forest soils are subject to severe erosion from
heavy rains. When the topsoil is washed away,
the remaining clay often bakes rock-hard in the
tropical sun.

120-121 *Fields of sugar cane usurp Costa Rican rainforest. In the rainforest, individual members of a species are dispersed through large areas of forest, making them less prone to pests and diseases. When a single crop is grown in large areas, however, it becomes an easy target for attack, and large amounts of chemicals are needed to protect plants from harm.*

122 Indonesian rainforest succumbs to burgeoning populations of peasant farmers. A majority of Indonesia's forest has already disappeared, with deforestation rates continuing to rise.

123 Cattle ranching has played a major role in Brazilian deforestation, with the beef raised there destined for the world's fast food restaurants.

124 A bird catcher in Peru takes some conures toward captivity. A large percentage of birds and reptiles captured from the forest die before reaching their destinations in foreign pet stores.

125 Plantation agriculture is another culprit in rainforest destruction. Tropical nations, desperate for foreign exchange, turn to their land to produce crops for export to the industrialized world.

126 The wasteland of Madagascar's central plateau brings home the reality of the consequences of deforestation. There is an urgent need to protect the world's remaining forests from further destruction.

127 A strip mine scars the tropical landscape. Many rainforests, particularly those in the Amazon Basin, are threatened by development of the resources that lie beneath them. The Amazon harbors the largest iron ore deposit in the world, at Carajas.